So, Your Child Wants to go to DRAMA SCHOOL

Everything **YOU** need to know when your child decides to chase their dream.

AMANDA B. COSGROVE

Copyright © 2020 Amanda B. Cosgrove

All rights reserved.

This publication or any portion thereof, may not be reproduced or used in any manner whatsoever without the express permission of the author.

Whilst the author has made every effort to ensure that the ideas, guidelines, and information presented in this book are completely reliable, they should be used at the reader's discretion.

The author cannot and will not be held responsible for any personal or commercial damage arising from the application or misinterpretation of the information presented herein.

ISBN: 9-798647-67160-8

CONTENTS

Foreword - Alex James-Hatton   Page 7

Introduction - Amanda B. Cosgrove   Page 9

1. The Conversation   Page 12
"I Want to go to Drama School"
"Ok - But What's Your Plan B?"

2. The Application   Page 19
What Does Your Child Actually Want to Do?
Which School?
Which Course?
Open Days
Graduation Performances & Showcases
The Application
The Audition Fees
The Personal Statement

3. The Preparation   Page 38
What to Prepare - The Student
What to Prepare - The Parent
Mindset & Expectations

4. The Audition   Page 45
Audition Day Top Tips

5. The Outcome   Page 49
The Cut
The Recall
and sometimes...An Interview

6. The Decision   Page 54
Waiting
No
No, However…

Yes, However…
Yes

7. The Realisation — Page 61
It's a Yes!
Continuing the Process
Securing the Place

8. The Funding — Page 66
How Much Do You Need?
Student Loans
DaDa's, Scholarships & Bursaries
Applying for Funds Elsewhere
Fundraising Ideas
Working
Keeping Track of Your Finances

9. The Move — Page 89
Connecting with Others
Accommodation
Finding a Part-Time Job
Starter Kit

10. The Beginning — Page 98
Freshers
Day 1
Conclusion

The Appendix — Page 107
25 Drama Schools
Schools Currently Offering Dance & Drama Awards
Helpful Funding Websites
Links to Non-School Related Bursaries
Sample Personal Statement
Example Starter Kit Requirements
Sample Funding Application Letter
Performing Arts CV
Links to Other Useful Websites

DEDICATION

For my late parents, with thanks for their lifelong encouragement and unconditional support.

FOREWORD

Over the years, I've seen many friends give up on pursuing a career in acting, musical theatre, or dance, purely because of the negative reactions of their parents or guardians. Having to hear things like: 'Ridiculous course fees' or, 'London's scary and expensive' or, 'Why don't you get a proper degree?'.

It's so upsetting.

I wish they'd had this book.

This is a crucial read and the only one I know, that has been especially written for parents rather than students. I can guarantee it's one that you won't find anywhere else... trust me I've tried.

When I began my journey and first told my mum I wanted to audition, she was of course nervous. Nervous at the thought of trying to find the money whilst supporting me through the most intense training of my life so far.

I'm lucky because she was awesome. Even so, there was so much we didn't know, and we had no choice but to learn the hard way. You, on the other hand, have it relatively easy as it's all written down for you here, in this book.

The book will soon become your best friend, as it takes you on the journey from the initial conversations to the big day itself. With information on applications, auditions, funding, moving out, and everything else in between.

Here, you will find all the answers for people who know what they're doing but really have no idea what's to come, and those who honestly wouldn't know where to begin.

This handy guide is crammed with gems, which I just wish my mum and I had known before I auditioned. It is crucial, insightful, calming, and extremely user-friendly.

I'm now living my dream and proof that it can be done. Two years out of training and I've performed in original West End casts, touring casts, and you can even hear me on an original cast recording!

But none of it would have happened without my mum. And funnily enough, she's the one who's written this book... Enjoy!

Alex James-Hatton (Actor)

INTRODUCTION

It's all very well me telling you that I was trained in dance from the age of 4, and was a member of a prolific theatre company, where I acted, directed, choreographed, made costumes, and even worked in the theatre bar. It is probably irrelevant that I went on to teach dance and choreograph numerous musical theatre productions.

It's perhaps *slightly* more relevant that I went on to open my own Musical Theatre Academy, which has since become award-winning and that I run a talent management company. *However,* the thing I am most proud of is being a parent and supporting my son up to drama school, through it and out the other side.

It came as no surprise, that after years of taking my son along to various rehearsals and shows, that he had caught the performing arts bug, and eventually, became fully immersed in everything theatrical. It was also no surprise to me that he ultimately wanted to forge a career as an actor, which in turn, meant going to drama school.

Although I understood his desire more than many parents, the prospect of dealing with the whole drama school process was daunting and the road ahead looked pretty scary, especially the funding.

Together we researched for hours and made our way through the maze of open days, applications, auditions, and funding. The process was stressful at times but invaluable, and it's the reason I can write this book.

I have physically and emotionally been through everything that you are about to undertake. We made mistakes, argued, and cried, but we made it through to the end, and it gives me immense pride to say that my son is now a professional actor.

It's only with this hindsight that I have been able to sit down and put my experience on paper. The resulting book is packed with information to guide you and your child through the complete process. It is written with affection for something that, at the time, was both stressful yet exciting but has only left fond memories.

I have done all the research, so you don't have to, and you'll find an appendix full of gems to help you manage any tricky corners. I recommend having a highlighter at the ready and be prepared to scribble down your thoughts as you make your way through the pages. I've included some blank templates for extra notes, and I'd encourage you to make photocopies - you'll need them!

In short, please look upon these pages, as the tools you'll need to enable your child to learn their chosen trade.

I wish them (and you) every success.
Amanda

CHAPTER 1
THE CONVERSATION

"I Want to go to DRAMA SCHOOL!"

Hopefully, by now, you'll have had some indication that your child is interested in pursuing a career in the performing arts industry, *before* you hear those immortal words, and if this *is* the first time you've heard them, then you need this book more than you first thought!

Before we go any further, I encourage you to have an open and honest conversation about your child's chances.

You may be surprised to hear that every UK drama school receives roughly 3000 to 6000 applications per year with usually, only 30-50 places available per school. That small intake is going to leave a lot of very disappointed auditionees, and, if your child is a girl, unfortunately, her chances are even slimmer!

Ask yourself the following questions and be totally honest with your replies.

1. Has your child ever shown an interest in performing?

2. Can they *actually* sing, dance, or act? Or are at least showing some potential?

3. Do they regularly change their mind about what they want to be?

4. Were they going to be an optician last week and a vet the week before? Perhaps a footballer or a chef? *

If the answer is yes, I politely suggest you return this book for a refund!

In short, what have they ever done to make you or themselves think they can do this? The word 'hunger' comes to mind. In someone that wants to act, sing, or dance as a living, they need to show hunger. Not just passion, it's more than that. Having a hunger means they will go above and beyond to reach their goal and it should be almost palpable.

In my case, my son had been a member of a local theatre academy, had singing lessons, had sang in a youth choir, had taken part in school productions, played the guitar and had written songs, etc. He had known from an early age that he wanted to work in the performing arts industry in some form or another. (although he did very nearly study pop music and song writing instead of the Musical Theatre course he eventually chose).

With all of the above in mind, has your child done any of the following:

1. Actively taken part in school productions?

2. Belonged to the school choir or a local singing group?

3. Attended drama classes, singing lessons or has had dance tuition?

4. Is, or has previously been, a member of a local theatre school or amateur dramatic society?

5. Followed a musical theatre website or blog, scouring YouTube for anything remotely theatre or performance related?

6. Regularly visited the theatre and collected theatre programmes? (more about programmes later)

If the answer to any of these questions is yes, then the chances are that you are about to start a stressful but exciting journey and you should keep reading!

Some students may have already sat GCSE and/or A-Level drama exams or perhaps a BTEC Performing Arts course. Others may have already auditioned for, or participated in, The National Youth Theatre or National Youth Music Theatre productions that take place all over the UK.

If your child is one of these students, you already know that it's what they want to do. (If they haven't, I've popped some useful links in the appendix for you).

At this stage, it's really important to point out that your child *can* still succeed without this mass of experience. Some people have an innate gift, and your child may well be one of them. With careful research and applications to the right schools, there is no reason why your child can't get into a drama school.

The creatives on the audition panels can spot natural ability a mile off. They are not interested in what your child has already done, but what they *can* do in the future with the school's help, guidance, and specialist training. There is nothing quite so special as finding someone with raw talent, so go for it!

Once you agree that your child is going to follow their dream, there is one important thing I have to tell you… under no circumstances utter the following words:

"Ok - But What's Your Plan B?"

It's my personal opinion, but I strongly believe that this is the dreaded phrase that comes before failure!

If your child is as determined as they are making out, then they absolutely do not want to think about a 'Plan B'. All it does is indicate to them that they might not achieve their dream, and this particular dream requires total commitment.

Anyway, why would you even give them an option? You have just agreed to support them on their journey. There is no room for a Plan B. In fact, there is just one plan you'll be following from now on and you have to be prepared to commit to it **100%**

I'm sad to say that all too often I have seen talented young performers get excited about auditioning and have been prepared to put in 100% effort, only to fail when their families or parents don't have the same level of commitment.

I can't stress it strongly enough.

Parents, your child needs you for this.

They will look to you for encouragement, help with applications, lifts to the train station, and of course, money...let's not forget the money!

Money! As soon as drama school tuition fees are discussed, panic sets in. Can you really afford to send them to drama school? Surely it costs thousands of pounds.

The short answer is...YES!

Well, at least it *can* do. The top conservatoires in the UK *are* expensive, but please, don't let that scare you off just yet.

Where there's a will, there is always a way and, there are many, many schools offering fantastic courses at affordable fees these days.

You *can* do this.

More about money later, but for now, let's continue...

CHAPTER 2
THE APPLICATION

What Does Your Child Actually Want to Do?

There are many disciplines within the arts. Is your child clear about where their strengths lie and what they actually want to do?

Here are some suggestions:

1. Musical Theatre
2. Acting
3. TV/Film Acting
4. Dance
5. Directing

The answer to this question will determine the schools they eventually apply to. If they already attend a college, amateur theatre company, or stage school, those organisations can usually help point them in the right direction. In the meantime, here is a brief explanation of what's involved in each type of course:

Which Course?

Musical Theatre

This is often referred to as 'Triple Threat Training' because intense training is offered in acting, singing, and dancing. Skills, technique, and performance will be looked at in detail and will be displayed at the end of year performances, when industry agents are invited to attend.

There is a small amount of written work, however, the emphasis is on performance and audition technique. Students on this type of course generally want to perform in musicals but are considered actors, and employment is found in all areas of the industry including, stage, film, and television.

Acting
This course is for those who want to *intensely* study the art of acting. There is sometimes a little singing and dancing, but this needn't be the student's strength.

Like the Musical Theatre course, there is a small amount of written work, but the emphasis is on performance and audition technique. Students on this course generally want to act for stage, film, and television.

Acting for TV/Film
Some schools offer this course separately from their 'Acting' course. It is much more specific than the general acting course with the intent of enabling employment in the TV/Film industry as opposed to the stage. The techniques are very different but

are also covered in the acting course. Choosing this option might increase the chances of employment in this field, but be aware, it might narrow the chances of future stage work.

Dance

Usually, there is no singing required and there will be opportunities to look at acting through dance. A 'dance only' course is for students who have generally danced for many years and are ballet trained, but this isn't set in stone.

Schools look for natural ability and potential in their students. The physical body also needs to have a natural facility for dance. In other words, with the correct body proportion, hip rotation, ankle flexibility, height of the foot instep, arch etc. the body would facilitate the ability to dance given the correct training.

A specifically designed dance course could include ballet, jazz, contemporary, tap, street, commercial, and sometimes, acrobatics.

Directing

Please be aware that most 'Directing' courses are actually postgraduate degrees and applicants will most likely have a degree in acting, dance, or musical theatre already. If this is the direction they wish to follow, encourage your child to look at those options first.

If your child is more interested in getting involved behind-the-scenes, there are many production and stage management courses available.

Unfortunately, those aren't the focus of this book, as they don't involve an audition process (although an interview is required). Application is usually via UCAS and details of the courses can be found on the individual websites.

Now you have some idea of the types of courses available, the next dilemma is knowing *where* to study.

Which School?

There are three different types of school available:

University
When your child declares a desire to attend a drama school, the traditional university route is *not* what they meant. A traditional university offering drama as a degree course is not a drama school, however, it doesn't mean you should rule it out.

At university, the drama courses focus on the academic side of the subject as well as the performance.

However, the good news is, that there are no auditions, a full student loan should be available to cover all the tuition fees and there will be halls of residence available to the students, so the headache of private rental won't be an issue.

Should your child be unsuccessful in auditioning for their preferred drama school, a university course is still something to consider. Getting a degree in Drama is a great starting point for anyone wanting to work in the industry and offers a gateway for many jobs within that industry other than performing. (Teaching, writing, producing, running a dance school, starting a theatre company, etc.)

Universities offering specialist training
These *are* considered to be drama schools and although the specialist courses are among many other courses being offered on the campus, they do offer the professional, vocational training necessary for entry into the industry, and an audition is required.

The tuition fees are usually the same as traditional universities, (sometimes a little more) and you'll be relieved to know that full funding is often available to you.

Accommodation is nearly always available, so this choice ticks all the boxes from both student and parent angles. If your biggest fear when your child mentioned drama school, was the funding, (call me psychic, but I think it was!) then this can be a fabulous route to take.

Conservatoires
These are the schools that everyone wants to go to and I doubt your child will feel any different. They are the leaders in the industry and offer training, opportunities, contacts, and connections that are second to none.

However, these opportunities come at a cost and it is these schools that charge much higher fees than the universities, but in return, the number of actual contact hours is much higher. They are the hardest schools to get into and students will undergo a rigorous audition process before being accepted or rejected. More on this later.

It takes hours and hours of research to find all the information that you'll need before starting applications, and I strongly suggest that your child does this before going much further.

However, just in case they don't do this or choose not to share this information with you, I've researched 25 drama schools/specialist university courses around the UK and provided the information required to make an initial application.

I've compared fees, types of courses, and even provided a selection of notable alumni because let's be honest, that's something us parents want to know! And it's all at the back of this book.

But wait! Before you start to trawl through all that information, I'd like you to consider the following:

1. **Which school offers the course that suits them best?**
   This roughly translates to - Which course is fully funded? (good luck in trying to convince your child that's the school for them!)

2. **How far are they willing to travel?**
   Or, how far are you willing to drive back and forth for the next 3 years?

3. **Does the school offer scholarships or bursaries?**
   Get on your knees and pray!

4. **How much is the audition fee?**
   Yes, you have to pay to audition… every time… every school.

5. **Not to mention the tuition fees!**
   Don't panic, there's a whole chapter on this!

6. **Will they leave with an actual degree**?
   Yes, but it sometimes costs a little extra (see the appendix).

The list could easily go on and on.

I mentioned earlier that your child should still do their own research. I highly recommend this because it will give them a real feel for each school, which is incredibly important. After all, the course has got to be a good fit for them.

Open Days

One of the best ways for your child to decide whether a school feels right for them is to attend an open day. Most schools have them, certainly all the university-based courses do. Not all the conservatoires do, as they consider their intense audition days an ideal opportunity to get a good feel for the school.

Open days give your child the opportunity

to attend various seminars and if the school has on-site accommodation, they usually provide a tour, so take the time to go on one.

Take a good look around the local town centre too, grabbing some lunch at the local pub if funds allow, or have a picnic in the local park and watch the world go by. This will give you a really good feel for a place. It's no good applying for the course your child likes the best if they are not going to feel safe and will want to come home after two weeks!

Graduation Performances & Showcases

This is time incredibly well spent. Not only can you see the standard of the emerging talent and get an understanding of how good you need to be, but you will also see the effectiveness of the training provided. These productions are attended by industry professionals and agents, so it's about as good as it gets until they perform professionally.

I personally found that the schools varied enormously. Not necessarily better or worse, but different. One school was very creative and experimental, and another very sleek and polished. This experience really does encompass everything you need to know about the school.

At the performance or showcase, there will usually be a programme available. This will include, amongst other things, headshots, and believe it or not, these can provide an insight into who the school is looking for.

Some things to look out for are the male/female split of that year's intake and the range of ethnicities represented. Ask yourself, 'Would my child feel at home in this building? 'It will certainly give you some food for thought!

In addition to the obvious benefits gained, in watching the graduates perform, this is a great time for a parent and their child to spend quality time together and to gain a mutual understanding of what the child is looking for in a course.

Once you have both experienced a feel for the schools your child wants to apply to, it's time to submit the applications, pay the audition fees (yes, the outgoings start here), and write a personal statement.

Let's look at each one of these:

The Application

Application forms will have to be submitted either by post or online and will either be direct to the drama school or via UCAS (The Universities and Colleges Admissions Service). UCAS is usually used when the course you're applying for is at a university rather than a conservatoire, (the privately-run drama school, with higher fees).

Sometimes, you'll be required to apply to both UCAS *and* the school, but don't worry, I've made this clear in the appendix.

Be sure to make a note of the school 'institution code' found on their website. You'll need this if you ever apply for a student loan. I learned this from experience as we were told time and time again that the school, we had chosen wasn't supported by the student loan system. It was only by producing the institution code that we finally had confirmation that it *was* an eligible school.

I haven't listed them in the appendix as you will also need the course code which varies from course to course. When you're ready, check the individual website for the codes. The websites, *are* of course, in the appendix!

Although it's not widely admitted, please apply early.

This applies mainly to the conservatoires. Auditions are usually held between October/November to March/April and places are offered approximately a week after each audition session, so it stands to reason that by the time you reach April, many of the places have already been taken.

Of course, every drama school will tell you that this has been taken into consideration, but why take the risk. Get your child to apply early and grab one of the first audition sessions. The only downside to this is that they will have less time to prepare, but it certainly gives them a kick to get on with it!

You will find that each school will request slightly different information at the initial stage. Some ask for photographs, usually just a headshot, but sometimes a full length shot and occasionally (especially schools specialising in dance), photos in certain dance positions. (an arabesque for example).

Other schools require references (I suggest their music teacher from school or a singing/dance teacher), and nearly all of them want a personal statement. More on this in a moment, and there is also a sample personal statement in the appendix.

Audition Fees

Audition fees (some schools call it an application fee) differ from school to school and occasionally there can be an additional recall fee.

The majority of auditions are held at the drama school concerned, although more and more schools in the UK are going out to regional colleges for the first round of auditions, or to major regional venues. Oh yes… I forgot to tell you, there will usually be more than one round… sometimes there are three.

Most schools hold their auditions between October and March, with recalls following in April and May. Although be aware that a few schools audition into June. It can be a long process, so if you are intending on accompanying your child to the various auditions, (not all parents do) be prepared to fill in your diary and book those dates off work.

Suggest to your child to start a notebook or file on each school and keep everything together as it will make life easier. Remember to include the prospectus, fee information, map of how to get there, the lot. (of course, this is for you just as much as it's for them, but I'm trying to encourage some independence here!)

The cost of auditioning varies, so I have included this information in the appendix for you, but please also be aware that some schools will waive this fee if the student is from a lower-income family. It's worth taking a look at the school's website to see if your child can benefit from this.

Remember, they will probably audition for several schools, so it soon adds up!

Personal Statement

A personal statement supports the student's application. It's a chance for them to articulate why they'd like to study a particular course or subject, and what skills and experience they possess that display their passion for their chosen school and course.

Most schools require a personal statement and it is usually limited to around 500 words. It is important that your child uses this opportunity to create a real impact and stand out from the crowd. Be the flamingo in the flock of pigeons!

There is an art to writing a personal statement and it doesn't start with "I have been interested in performing since I was three".

This is your child's opportunity to tell the school about their experience and to mention a few things such as... well... remember that list from earlier?

1. Their school productions

2. Their school choir and concerts

3. Their drama classes, singing lessons, and dance tuition

4. Their theatre school or amateur dramatics society

5. The musical theatre websites, blogs and the hours they've spent scouring YouTube

6. Their theatre visits and don't forget those theatre programmes getting dusty next to the PlayStation

Speaking of those theatre programmes, here's where they come into their own. Get your child to sit down with as many programmes as they can find and highlight the schools that the various cast members studied at.

It is interesting to see which shows use which schools. There is usually a reason for this. A show that is 'ballet heavy' may use actors that have trained at specialist dance school for example. Your child will also be able to see which schools are currently getting its students' work. It's a useful tip and can be quite inspiring too.

If your child has not been able to attend many theatre productions, (because let's face it ticket prices can be extortionate), suggest that they look at the cast lists online. Every show has its own website and full casts lists are usually displayed.

Anyhow, back to the personal statement. *Here are some ideas to help your child get started:*

1. They should look at course descriptions and identify the qualities, skills, and experience required. They can then ensure that they mention these qualities in their statement.

2. They should tell the school why they are applying – highlight their ambitions, as well as what interests them about the subject or the course.

3. They should think about what makes them suitable – this could be relevant experience, skills, or achievements they've gained from education, work, or other activities.

4. They could include any clubs or societies they belong to – sporting, creative, or musical.

5. They can mention any relevant employment experience or volunteering they've done, such as The Duke of Edinburgh Award.

6. Nearly everyone will include the information mentioned previously, and some will attach a full CV of their theatre experience (guilty)! This is fine, but please also include something refreshing like:

   - Which Composer they currently admire and why
   - What they are hoping to learn from this particular course.
   - What qualities do they possess that will help them excel at drama school.

Remember, that this is *also* about being punctual, polite, hardworking, not giving up, and giving more than the required 100% and this should come across loud and clear. Hopefully, you get the gist!

Basically, all of the above greatly expanded and then edited down to approximately 500 words. No pressure! Fortunately, a full example is available to you in the appendix (you're welcome!).

Be prepared for your child to argue with you over the personal statement because whatever you say will be different from the advice given from their college, and that will differ from their friend, who got in previously, and so on.

All you can do is let them write it and proofread it for them. At least you now know what to look out for and hopefully, you can take guidance from the above suggestions and enclosed examples.

By the way, unless you have an older or more independent child, I suspect you might be the one who will be printing off multiple copies of the statement and posting them. Either way, a word of advice - every time you send a new copy, make sure that you change the name of the school, especially if you've used it in the statement at the top of the letter.

Eventually, an audition will be offered... After all, you've paid them £50 for the privilege!

CHAPTER 3
THE PREPARATION

What to Prepare - The Student

This section sounds like it should be for your child to read, but actually, they should already know this… remember all that research?

However, in case they don't keep you in the loop, here's a quick outline of what might be required. Be mindful that each school has slightly different requirements, so make sure your child has prepared correctly. Usually you can expect something along the following lines:

ACTING
1 x Shakespeare/Classical Monologue
1 x Contemporary Monologue (Usually pre-1979)

(Each monologue should be chosen themselves and be no longer than 2 minutes and generally, spelling should be appropriate for your child's age and gender and almost certainly performed in your their own accent, unless specified otherwise).

SINGING
1 x Contemporary musical theatre song - Usually post 1980
1 x Legit musical theatre song - Usually pre 1980

(Both songs to be chosen themselves).

DANCING

More often than not, auditions start with dance which normally consists of a warm-up, general jazz class and corner work. After this, a short routine will normally be taught and performed in small groups.

IMPORTANT:

Imagine how many songs and monologues the audition panel see every year! With this in mind, your child should be mindful of which ones they choose. There are highly accessible lists of 'overdone' songs and monologues available online and certainly worth a look. There are also many books written specifically for the student that cover this.

If they get recalled and are not cut at the first stage, they will get to display their talents in all three areas, but this isn't always the case. Most auditionees get cut after the dance round. Yep... harsh but true.

Some schools expect the student to attend an interview. This is when the superbly written personal statement comes into play. If your child made their statement up, they are about to get found out! Hopefully, though, they will have been clever and mentioned the latest piece of creative theatre they saw, or their current favourite composer, and be able to bang on about that! (obviously, thanks go to you for reading this book).

What to Prepare - The Parent

Do some homework on the school. The addresses and websites are all in the appendix for you, so no excuses.

Some questions to consider: Where is the nearest station? Is it within walking distance? Do you need to stay the night before? What hotel? Can you drive there? Where can you park?

On the subject of parking, especially in London, it can be a nightmare and will cause untold stress if left until the day. I advise using a site like Just Park (www.justpark.com). You can pre-book your parking space and choose exactly where you want to be. Your budding performer doesn't want to get blown to bits or soaking wet on a cold November audition day just because you parked miles away! Stress, stress, stress, and all easily avoidable.

Make sure they have all the clothes, dance-wear and shoes that are required. Have they taped their piano music correctly? (yes seriously!) And most important of all... is it all packed?

On the subject of piano music, I found a really great video on YouTube that clearly explains how to tape and present sheet music. It's well worth a look.

You can find a link to it in the appendix.

At this stage, your child will be up to their eyeballs with nerves, so if you can take care of some of the above then I'm sure it will be much appreciated.

Mindset and Expectations

Let's stop for a moment and consider what is about to happen? Remember that between 3000 and 6000 people will have applied for the course and there are only 30-50 places. It's important to be positive, however, there is a very real chance that your child will *not* be offered a place.

It is absolutely normal for them not to get in and most students will ultimately attend several auditions, sometimes for many years, and will never be offered a place. Rejection is a big part of this profession. As a performer, your child will experience rejection throughout their career, and no matter how famous or successful they become, (see how positive that was), it's part of the job.

With this in mind, please do not give up on your child after one 'No'. Reassure them that this is the name of the game and what doesn't kill you makes you stronger. Not getting into drama school is not the end of the world and it certainly doesn't mean that they are not good enough.

Your child can audition again next year and quite honestly, the year after that too if necessary - all depending on how much 'hunger' your child really has!

Stay positive, but realistic, and absolutely do not mention this to them on the actual audition day.
They probably already know exactly what their chances are and you reinforcing that isn't going to help.

A few years ago, I discovered something called 'Switch Words' They are words designed to help you manifest what you want. Now, I know this might not be to everyone's taste, but *we* found it to be really useful, especially with the handling of nerves.

This is how it works. If you say something over and over again, as you do with affirmations, your brain starts to believe it. The words you choose though are largely unrelated to the reason you've chosen them. E.g. BLUFF is the 'Switch Word' that helps dispel anxiety, fear, or nervousness, the word UP is for confidence and the word BUBBLE is meant to attract energy and to help you go beyond perceived limitations.

With this in mind, as your child nears their audition or any situation where they might feel anxious, try saying:

BLUFF - UP - BUBBLE

If they do this repeatedly, it can take their mind off the fear and because it actually sounds quite ridiculous, it lightens the mood.

Have a go. They're easy to use and worth a try. If nothing else you'll have a laugh!

Unfortunately, if I put a list of 'Switch Words' in the appendix I'd probably be sued, so take a look at the book yourself. I've included the details in the appendix.

CHAPTER 4
THE AUDITION

Audition Day Top Tips

These are based on my own experience with an audition in West London. I was in a position to be able to drive my son to London and to stay overnight (Although the hotel I chose was the cheapest I could find, and barely fit for purpose!) If you are able to go along, great, but if your child is going independently, don't worry, you are only at the end of a phone!

#1 – If you live some distance away, arrive the night before. This will do away with traffic headaches, last-minute weather issues, panics, or stressful arguments. Trust me when I say that your child will already be stressed out, so one of your jobs is to make things go as smoothly as possible.

An overnight stay also gives you the opportunity for a trial run to see where the drama school entrance is. But remember to book your hotel early, because all the show-biz mums have already done it! If an overnight stay isn't possible, just make sure you have researched your directions in advance and get the earliest train possible. The aim here is to arrive on the day less stressed.

#2 – The evening before (wherever you are), enjoy some food, chat through what will happen the following day and then do your best to get a good night's sleep. If your child travelled alone, advise them not to go out clubbing with any of the famous residents. (I know someone who actually did this.

She had a great time, but it wasn't exactly great audition preparation!) No of course I can't tell you who, but the local residents of this particular area at the time, included Stephen Mulhern, Richard Osman, Clare Balding, David Tennant, and Ant 'n Dec... I'll let you decide who it was!

#3 – Set your alarm early and get up in plenty of time. That means early enough for them to drink water, eat breakfast, drink more water, steam*, drink even more water, and do a vocal warm-up. If they don't want to sing in the hotel, suggest they go and prepare in the car or maybe they will feel brave enough to entertain the hotel guests at breakfast!

If your child is a singer, they should already be doing this regularly. It involves inhaling the steam from boiling water in order to clear the nasal passages and loosen the vocal cords. Much the same as putting your head over a bowl of menthol water when you have a head cold!

#4 – Have plenty of tissues in your pocket! Leave the hotel for the audition and say farewell to your baby as they enter the building.

Be prepared for the tears – yours and theirs! This is one time you can't do it for them... it's up to them now!

#5 – As you blink through your tears, take care not to bump into oncoming auditionees who have only just arrived and got lost, or left their tap shoes on the train or have just woken up with a hangover because last night they bumped into...Insert who you think it was here!

It is worth mentioning, that many parents I have spoken to who have already been through this process have actually really enjoyed it. It gives you quality time with your child and you get to see new cities.

I suggest you embrace these days out and get as much as you can from them. Once again though, please don't stress if you are unable to go or your child doesn't want you to go. Your thoughts will be with them all day and I'm positive there will be more than one phone call home for whatever the reason!

Once the audition has finished... Now what?

You wait... until they have been cut (ouch!) or recalled (yay!) Read on for the next stage....

CHAPTER 5
THE OUTCOME

The Cut

First of all, don't panic. There was a 99% chance that this was going to happen. I did warn you. So, what do you do next? Actually, you do have a choice here.

Option A:
Console them with something nice to eat and drink and talk it through. Apart from anything else, this will make the most of your trip to London or wherever you are, but there are a few things to consider.

A whole load of others just got 'cut' too, and the local streets are full of them. It's probably not what your child wants to see right now. Nearly every 18 plus student walking past your carefully chosen posh cafe window, already attends said drama school and the sight of these talented and successful chosen ones, will be too much to bear.

No matter what you say, it'll be wrong. Your child has just been told they are not good enough... this time. Their world has just fallen apart. *You* know there will be other opportunities and other auditions and even other jobs, but that's NOT what they want to hear right now!

Option B:
Head straight back to the car after giving them a quick hug and telling them that the school doesn't know what it's missing.

Back to the motorway, turn up the tunes and stop at the services for a burger. They will probably 'fall asleep' to avoid communication at this point, but that's fine, you don't know what to say anyway!

The Recall

After several hours you will find yourself outside the school with dozens of other parents. As most auditions are held in the Winter, it will most likely be freezing cold while you eagerly await your little darling to appear through the double doors.

Suddenly, out they come. Some on their own and others in small groups. You watch as they pair up with their parents or friends and slowly drift off to the local cafés and service stations. But your child hasn't appeared yet. Do you wait for longer? Have you missed them? Don't tell me they've been… and then out they bound, grinning like a Cheshire cat.

"I've been recalled. I'm going straight back in. You can find something to do for another couple of hours, can't you?"

What!? Of course, you can!

Is this actually happening? So, it's not just you that thought they could do it! Cue more tears… more tissues.

I hope you like hot chocolate because you are about to drink eight of them over the next few hours, and all in different cafes.

On the bright side, you can always kill some time in the local book shop, but realistically, how long can you browse around Waterstones without actually buying anything or looking like a shoplifter!

And Sometimes, an Interview

Eventually, you slowly make your way back to the school, unsure if you've estimated the waiting time correctly. And then your baby suddenly appears. They explain that after the recall there was an interview and now, they have to wait a whole week for the answer!

> *Sorry did you say an interview?*
> *This is excellent news and very promising.*

But for now, it's back in the car and there's no time for 'tunes' because you want the ins and outs of *everything,* and your child can't talk quickly enough! Of course, there will be a brief chance to catch a breath for that service station burger… but this time it's celebratory!

CHAPTER 6
THE DECISION

Waiting

The letter, or email usually arrives a week or two after the final audition. Yet, despite knowing this, you will both be running to the letterbox upon the faintest sound of the postman's approach and checking your emails every 2 minutes!

Prepare yourself for a very long and tense wait!

Finally, after what feels like an eternity, the letter drops on the mat or your email notification pings! Your child may want to read this in private, so be prepared to give them space to do so but then stand nearby and wait with bated breath.

Take this time to work on that face you see at the Oscars when the nominees don't win!

Yes, let's be real, it might be that despite a recall and an interview and a week's wait for the outcome, it's still a 'NO', so, what next?

Actually, there are 4 possible outcomes:

NO

A big fat definite no. To be clear, this means, no feedback, no explanation, and most definitely no offers. Zilch, Nada, Nothing. NO!

Time to start the whole process again but be assured that this *is* normal.

If the thought of this makes your child ill, I'll tell you now, this industry is not for them. Your child has to be prepared to throw rejection aside and push through. This 'no' may potentially be the first of many.

Let's put a positive spin on this. Not getting in, actually offers a wonderful opportunity for them to improve their skills further. Working on their acting, singing, or dance skills for another year will increase their chances of giving a better audition next time, as well as showing the school that they are dedicated and have the guts to return for another chance to nail it.

They should use the next year to:

1. Visit the theatre and collect more theatre programmes to study!

2. Read plays, scripts, and books on acting. Perhaps a book on positive thinking or audition technique?

3. Work on their weakest area - If it's dance, take dance classes or watch dance tutorials online. If it's acting, there are some great interviews on YouTube by actors like Michael Caine, who impart fabulous advice. If singing is not their greatest strength, they could work on their vocal health by doing vocal exercises every day.

4. Get some life experience. Literally learn and experience new things and push their boundaries.

5. Observe people - People watching will give them superb references when they are next working on a new character.

6. Work. Your child can get a part job for a whole year and save like mad in order to pay for those eventual tuition fees!

NO (However...)

"Although not successful on this occasion, we would like to see you again next year and invite you to attend the recall stage of the audition process."

This is very positive and shouldn't be sniffed at.

It means that your child has shown potential, but the panel didn't feel it was quite the right time for them. It's possible that they have to gain a little more experience, or it may be that they already have enough boys or girls for that particular year's quota.

So re-apply. They have every right to feel smug and relieved because they won't have to go through the first round again.

Make sure that your child applies nice and early next year, as they stand a better chance of getting an earlier audition. The longer they leave it, the fewer places will be left. Don't say I didn't warn you!

But what if the letter says 'YES'. That's fantastic!

Except, there are also two types of yes...

YES (However...)

"We would like to offer you a place on our foundation course."

Ok, so this isn't the three-year course that they wanted, but it's a great start. Their talent has been recognised and they should be feeling really proud of themselves. This is in fact, a one-year course and there are pros and cons to consider:

PROs
1. They have clearly shown potential.

2. A year's worth of training will improve their skills even more.

3. They get a year to try the school before committing to the full 3 years.

4. It's an opportunity to see if it's what they really want to do

CONs
1. It costs. These are fees that could be saved for the following year! The fees are usually around the £10,000 mark, although student loans are currently available, and you can borrow for four years' worth of training including the foundation year.

2. Your child will *not* be guaranteed a place next year just because they have done the foundation course. This is *not* a fast pass.

YES

It says YES… Read it again to be sure… It still says YES… Read it again whilst dancing around the hall (in my case it was my works' staff room and he had ran all the way to work to show me!)… It still says YES.

Cry!

CHAPTER 7
THE REALISATION

It's a Yes

It's a Yes! A full-blown "you have been accepted on our 3 year course" type of yes!

You've screamed, danced around the room, phone calls have been made, text messages sent and possibly a 'bubbly' cork popped! If you're lucky enough to have a glass bubbly, enjoy it to the full, it may well be the last one you can afford until graduation!

And then here come the tears. Tears of joy, tears of pride, and finally, the realisation tears.

Hold on a minute… isn't this the school that's actually a conservatoire? Yep, they've got into the one that's *not* funded! Ouch!

So, what next?

Here's the thing. A la Charlie Bucket, do you accept the golden ticket, or do you wait to see if they get into any other schools? (funded ones for example!) Let's discuss…

Continuing the Process

Your child should by all means carry on auditioning. You've probably paid the audition fees upfront anyway, so they might as well, and wouldn't it be nice to say that they 'got in' to several schools and had a choice of offers?

However, keep in mind that every audition might cost you overnight accommodation, petrol or train fares and don't forget that service station burger!

This is totally up to you and your child, but let me share my experience. My son got into his first choice of school; however, it wasn't necessarily mine. Why? In a word, money. The school he wanted to go to was £14,500 per year at the time, and even with him sharing his accommodation with three others, the house rental, where the school was situated, was extortionate.

The school *I* liked and wanted him to go to would have been totally covered by a student loan! The on-campus accommodation was clean and reasonable, the area was lovely and there was even a lake to learn your lines by, so as far as I was concerned, it was a no brainer?

Right?

Wrong!

We ended up going with the first one. The expensive one and, in our opinion at the time, the best one. Having thoroughly done our research, visited the school, checked out the area (remember all those hot chocolates and nearly getting arrested in Waterstones for vagrancy?), we both felt it was a perfect choice and the best place to be.

Securing the Place

I want to be totally honest here, if they have got into their top choice and their top choice just happens to be the best school available, then take it. This is such a huge achievement and as scary as it seems, somehow you will make it work.

Accept the place, cancel all future auditions, and pay the deposit* before the school changes its mind.

The only drawback with this decision is that occasionally, I have seen people accept their place and then change their minds later. If your child is still undecided at the 'deposit paying' stage, give the school a call and arrange to pay the deposit later... it can be done.

*Yes, you have to pay a deposit, usually around £300-£600 and it's non-refundable.

Congratulations... your child is going to drama school!

CHAPTER 8
THE FUNDING

How Much Do You Need?

Now the hard work begins, not just for the child but for the family too. Parents, siblings, grandparents, the lot. They may not know it yet, but they all have a role to play and may be affected by this massive decision.

So... How much will you need?
Have you considered everything?

1. Tuition Fees (remember that's three terms for three years)

2. Dance-wear, tap shoes, jazz shoes, ballet shoes etc.

3. Books & Stationery

4. House Rental

5. House Bills: Gas, Electric, WIFI, etc.

6. Food

7. Transport (Buses/Tubes/Taxis etc.)

8. Travel to/from home at holiday times

First of all, you may well be in the fortunate position of having the funds you need. In which case, you should absolutely pay for the tuition directly to the school and avoid loans and the interest that is piled on top!

Unfortunately, I was certainly not in this position, so along with many others, my first point of call was to see how much of the course could be funded by a student loan.

Student Loans

Student loan funding differs depending on where you live, and the amount offered differs considerably between schools and courses. How will you know what courses are available and what the tuition fees are? Because I've done all the hard work for you… just turn to the appendix!

As a rule of thumb, if your child is going to university, they should be able to get a full student loan to cover their fees and, if they are eligible for student finance, they should also be able to make a claim for a maintenance loan. This is generally used to cover rent and living expenses.

Please remember, student finance is a *loan* and repayment is the responsibility of the student, *not* the parent. However, the good news is that, at the time of writing this book, they have to earn at least £25,725 (after tax) before any repayment is triggered.

Remember, (read this bit quickly like in the mortgage commercials)... there is interest payable on a student loan, which is currently 5.4%. This rate applies until the 5th of April after your child finishes their course or leaves the course. *(*Thank you for obliging!*)*

Once triggered, repayments will automatically be taken from their earnings. Let's hope this *does* happen because it means your talented actor has got a great job! Woo Hoo!

If your child is going to a conservatoire, they will only be eligible for a partial loan and this is usually around £6,000. Bear in mind that a conservatoire place costs approximately £15,000 a year, so this is only a small chunk of the full amount, but every little helps! The good news is that they should also be able to make a claim for a maintenance loan. At least they can rent a house to party in! Only joking. (not joking).

The maintenance loan is calculated by looking at where you live and your household income, but in addition to this, your child may be eligible for a maintenance *grant*. This is 'means-tested' so the amount will vary greatly from student to student.

In my case, both my partner and I worked, so my son got a grand total of £18. Yep, an £18 grant for the whole year. However, let's not knock it, remember, a grant isn't re-payable!

Depending on what part of the country you live in, the finance available will vary and there might be other forms of support available to you. i.e. a special support loan or a long course loan to name just two. I have provided links to the student finance sites for parts of the country, but a quick note for all of you in Northern Ireland.

There are no actual 'drama schools' in Northern Ireland itself, but you can study a BA(Hons) in Drama at two universities: Ulster University and Queen's University, Belfast. These do not form part of my drama school research in the appendix, as they are standard universities rather than specialist drama schools.

Take a look at the relevant site for your area and I am sure you find some useful information. You will probably feel much calmer, once you know what is available to you.

So, Things to remember:

1. There is usually a deadline for funding applications (see appendix) Write it in your diary!

2. The loan belongs to your child, not you.

3. Keep your child's Student Loan registration/reference number handy. In case your child loses it. Keep a file of all your applications, forms, passwords, etc. as you'll be accessing and using this information regularly throughout the three years.

4. There is a student loan, a maintenance loan and a grant available to you as well as possible DaDa's, Scholarships and Bursaries.

DaDa's, Scholarships and Bursaries

What's the difference?

A DaDa

I thought you'd never ask… a DaDa is a 'Dance and Drama Award.' The purpose of this award is to offer funding to students between the age of 16 and 23, who show exceptional talent and a likelihood to succeed in the industry.

The amount awarded depends on your household income and where they will live and study.

To be clear, it is means-tested and you and your child may not want to go through the invasive process. At the time of writing, there are about 17 schools that offer a DaDa. I have listed them in the appendix for you (obviously).

If your child is fortunate enough to be awarded a DaDa, congratulations, but please bear in mind that they will *not* be able to access the student loan system. This means no maintenance loan either, so they still have to find the funds for living expenses.

Of course, a DaDa is *not* a loan, so they have nothing to pay back. If they are awarded one, they will have to weigh up what's right for them. In some circumstances, a DaDa will cover *everything*, so if your child shows exceptional potential, despite not having experience or the funds, there is always hope!

A Scholarship
A Scholarship is provided on the basis of excellence and financial need may also be considered between candidates of equal achievement. Sometimes the students are automatically eligible for a scholarship when they accept their place and other times the

scholarship is auditioned for. Occasionally, there are several rounds to scholarship auditions.

A scholarship covers the tuition fees and is *not* repayable. Occasionally maintenance is covered too. If your child is awarded one of these, rejoice! You've hit the jackpot and they will not have to apply for a student loan.

Most schools offer scholarships, and, in many cases, they are offered *to* you rather than having to ask for one. They are awarded on the basis of the audition and the potential that the auditionee displayed.

A Bursary
Bursaries are often offered by the drama school and you will get a form to fill in and return at the start of each year. The school will assess whether your child is eligible for one. They will look at your financial needs, as well as their potential, attendance, etc.

Bursaries are often funded by alumni of the school or by local business angels, interested in the future of the theatre or upcoming talent.

Sometimes the donor of the bursary chooses a student to support, other times, the money comes from a big pot and is shared out to as many pupils as possible who qualify. The amounts offered are *very* varied.

If you are lucky enough to be awarded a bursary, that's great news, because a chunk of your fees will be paid, but be careful, as sometimes, only one bursary is allowed. If you've already received a bursary, you may not be eligible for another. Occasionally, if you're very fortunate, you will have to choose which bursary serves you the best.

It's also worth remembering that bursary money does not have to be paid back. It is essentially a non-repayable grant. However, if your child discontinues or takes a leave of absence from the course, a certain percentage may have to be repaid. Be warned!

Applying for Funds Elsewhere

Bursaries are also offered by private trusts, businesses, or entrepreneurs that are not linked to a specific drama school. Offers are based on the financial needs of the student and their family. (can you see a pattern forming here?) Occasionally an interview, and sometimes an audition is required to assess potential. You'll be required to complete an online or postal application for any of the major ones and again, there are strict deadlines. You have to be way ahead of the game to grab any of these.

To be absolutely honest with you, my son and I sent out about 50 letters/applications to private trusts and hardly got any responses. The problem wasn't our application form or letter, (in fact we had letters back that praised both of these, so I've popped a copy at the back!), but that the trusts had run out of funds or completely shut down.

We did eventually manage to secure some extra funding, but the donations came mainly from local schools, colleges, companies, and well-wishers that we already had connections with. Along with our local fundraising events, we managed to raise approximately £3000. This didn't make a massive dent in what we had to find, but it covered nearly a term's tuition and that's not to be sniffed at! My Son was also fortunate enough to win two bursaries over his three years at drama school, which was incredibly helpful.

If you do want to try the 'Private Trust' route, I have managed to find some links that still exist and will hopefully help you in your search for extra pennies! (a list is available to you in the appendix).

Let's presume that you still require additional funding and are going to try the various trusts listed at the back or you've decided to approach local business.

Where do you start?

Your child needs to write a strong letter that covers all the necessary points yet remains personal both to themselves and the company or trust they are approaching. They should attach a Theatrical CV to the back of the letter to show how much experience he or she has already had, along with a headshot, and remember to include a stamped addressed envelope. Without the latter, I doubt you will even get a response!

Regarding headshots. They'll need a decent photograph, but this doesn't mean you have to get it done professionally. You can save that expense for when they are at drama school. If your child is studying performing arts or drama at college, they will almost certainly have had a headshot taken as a matter of course, and they can use that. If not, a carefully posed photo using your mobile phone is fine. Make sure it is well lit and there is a plain background/wall behind them. The photo should be head and shoulders only and, at the moment, the trend is for coloured photographs not black and white. Once you're happy with the photograph, print out approximately six to an A4 page and this will be a good size to attach to the letter.

So, what should they say in the letter?
(If there isn't a formal application form to fill in.)

Start with a strong opening paragraph that is straight to the point and introduces themselves.

Next, they should talk about the drama school place that has been offered. This is their time to brag, remember he or she beat thousands to get that place.

Disclose the tuition fees and explain what you have already done to raise funds and what you are still intending to do. This is very important, as it shows how committed they are to their own cause. Think 'Dragons Den' when they ask how much of your own money you've put into the business!

Your child should tell the Trust a little about them self and mention any special awards or exceptional achievements. Perhaps they've already had some professional experience or attended workshops that gained them important experience or personal recommendations.

Remember that first conversation about how serious they were about auditioning? Dig it out and encourage your child to talk about their am-dram experience and school shows here. If they have already had private dance or singing lessons, include it, as it shows serious investment has already been made.

Finish with a killer paragraph or two that promises their commitment and how grateful they would be for the funding.

So now you get the idea! If only you had a sample letter to copy you could share... (you know where that is, right?)

Fundraising Ideas

Before delving deeper into fundraising, I feel you deserve a warning:

Most people support willingly, especially if the people you are asking to donate, have been a part of your child's education or life so far. However, if your child is going to a conservatoire, you may come across some strange reactions. People automatically think that because you are sending your child to what is in effect a private school, you must already have the money.

To be honest, this is totally understandable, and please don't get offended. Mr. Smith from next door doesn't know what's involved. Mrs. Brown from your spin class doesn't know how difficult it was to get into the school in the first place. Your sister doesn't realise how much the fees are, and your child's primary school teacher has probably forgotten who they are anyway.

Just be prepared for some strange comments along the way. *You* do understand and you're willing to sell your soul in order to get and keep your child there, so please don't take it personally, just keep going. Remember, the same people will want an autograph when your budding star is rich and famous! (Ha! Karma!)

Anyway, read on for some fundraising ideas:

Quizzes

Most people love a quiz. They are easy to organise and can be done anywhere, even online (Zoom, etc.) Each team pays £5 and the winners get a share of the money or a prize that you have cleverly negotiated from a local business e.g. a meal out, etc. They get a fun night out and you get some funds. **Win/Win.**

Local Restaurant Meal Deals
Loads of restaurants offer fundraising deals. For example, each person pays £10 and gets a choice from a limited menu offered by the restaurant. The room is full of your family, friends, and supporters. Half of the money pays for the meal and the other half goes into your pot. A great time is had by all. **Win/Win.**

Bucket Collections
WAIT! Do not shake! Apparently, it's against the law and classed as begging! However, if your child is in a show with an appreciative audience on hand, there is nothing to stop you placing a collection tin, bucket or hat at the exit.

You might be surprised at the amount collected… you might not. (I think we collected approx. £600). Anyway, the audience has enjoyed a great show (hopefully) and has voluntarily chosen to donate, so once again, you have a **Win/Win.**

Record and Sell a CD
If your child sings, consider recording a few tracks onto a CD and selling it for a reasonable sum… £5 is a good, affordable amount. Once again, the buyer gets a product and the funds go into the pot.

This is quite a nice one and actually, you might find

that some people will love the 'I supported them before they were famous' vibe! Yep... definitely a **Win/Win!**

Put on a Concert

Love this, it's just so showbiz! The chances are that your child belongs to an amateur dramatic society, theatre company, choir, etc. This is the time to get a few like-minded friends together and literally put on a show. You may need to hire a function room, theatre, or community centre for this, so make sure your ticket price covers your outgoings and still leaves a profit. So long as the audience gets a good night out, it's another **Win/Win.** (this is a really good one for press coverage from the local paper, which in turn might attract donations or further support).

Sing at Events

If your child sings, they should consider offering their services to local charity events in return for a donation. Some will pay properly for the privilege and others will expect it for free. They should attend all of these, after all, it's about raising their profile and you never know who will be in the audience.

My Son performed at an event at an old people's home and at the end I was approached by a lady who was interested in knowing more about him.

She happened to be the sister of the company principal of Laine Theatre Arts. At the time my son had already accepted an offer to another school, so nothing came of it, but doesn't it just show! You know what I'm going to say... **Win/Win.**

Run a Raffle

Now, believe it or not, this is actually quite a tricky one. I didn't realise until I undertook this process that raffles need to comply with the Gaming Commission and sometimes have to be registered with the local council!

The same person that made a sarcastic comment about you sending your child to a private school, will be the one, checking up on you, so get this right. Here's what you need to know:

Types of a raffle that do NOT require a licence

Small Raffle - The simplest raffle to organise and one which does not need to be registered with the Gambling Commission or Local Authority.

1. Tickets are only sold on the DAY OF THE DRAW, not before.

2. Tickets cannot cost more than £1.

3. A maximum of £250 only to be spent on prizes, but donated prizes can be accepted.

4. No money prizes can be offered, although gift vouchers are ok.

5. All proceeds must be donated to CHARITY. (This isn't you!).

Private Raffle - No need for registration of any sort.

1. Tickets may be sold to people living or working in the same premises, or who are members of an organisation or club.

2. This raffle may only be advertised on the tickets or to the people on the premises.

Types of a raffle that DO require a licence

Society Raffle - This kind of raffle needs to be registered with your local authority to obtain a licence and it is important they comply with the gaming commission.

1. A licence costs approx. £40 a year.

2. Tickets may be sold over a period of time.

3. Tickets may be sold to the general public

4. The maximum price you can charge for each ticket is £2

5. You must have a named promoter who is responsible for the draw. This can be a person or an organisation.

6. Tickets must not be sold to persons under the age of 16.

As you can see, it's quite a minefield, so unless you have been donated a holiday or a car that you can raffle, you will need to 'fit' your event around the *private* raffle model. Providing you do this properly, it's another **Win/Win.**

Crowdfunding

This is only my personal opinion and I am aware I might divide opinion with this one.

I know many people who have tried online fundraising/crowdfunding pages etc., but I feel that they are asking people to literally give them money in return for nothing. This is great for charities and we've all heard of Captain Tom Moore by now and his £30 million, but come on, you are not the NHS, you are not even a registered charity. Unless your story is super unusual and you have an excellent reason for asking for money for nothing, then I honestly wouldn't recommend it.

With this in mind, let me remind you of the previous point about sending your child to a private school - it won't always go down well and I've not yet seen a student raise a fortune this way... all those negative opinions for £50? I don't think so. **Lose/Lose.**

Working

Did you wonder when I was going to mention this? Your child is presumably aged between 16 - 20 and more than capable of getting a job of some sort.

They may still be studying; in which case a Saturday or evening job will do the trick and you'll be amazed how much they can save.

If they really want to follow their dream (and at this stage, you know they do), they shouldn't have a problem with taking a part-time job. You may, however, find that they come across a couple of obstacles along the way:

1. They are NOT available every Saturday, because they are involved in shows and rehearsals.

2. They can only work on Thursday nights, because the rest of the week, they have rehearsals, lessons, singing at events etc. (my fault!)

My son tried several jobs, but it was so hard to hold one down with all his amateur drama productions, concert rehearsals, and college work. Some shops loved him but wouldn't take him on because he couldn't do many shifts due to his commitments, whereas other places just didn't have the hours to suit him.

Although he didn't earn a huge amount, any money he did earn, certainly took the pressure off my income. He was able to pay for his own clothes, toiletries, the occasional football match ticket, and so on. It's not to be sniffed at. To be fair, he also used all his own savings to secure his dream of going to drama school, so hats off to him!

Keeping Track of Your Finances

At this juncture, we have to presume that enough money has been saved to fund the first year, or at the very least the first term and, time is starting to run out. If you haven't already done so, I suggest you start a finance sheet. This will keep track of what you need versus what you have. If you have access to an online spreadsheet (e.g. Excel) then it's a good idea to keep a running total.

Trust me, those tap shoes and dance belts add up!

Start with the amount that is currently available to you. This will include the student loan, maintenance loan, bursaries (if offered), grants, savings and funds raised at events, etc.

Then list all the outgoings, including tuition fees, house rental, travel, etc. Keep a live running total that shows your funds depleting as time goes on. If unexpectedly you get a donation or a bursary from one of your many applications, simply add it in along the way.

This can be a scary process, so if you want to keep your sanity, a good idea is to break it down per term or per year rather than the whole three years.

There are a few things to remember:

1. A student loan is usually paid directly to the school or university, so it won't ever hit *your* bank account.

2. A maintenance loan will go to your child's bank account because it is *their loan*. In my case, I have to admit, that I transferred the funds to an unused savings account I had, and called this his 'Drama School' account. This account was used for everything drama school related. This is a wise move, as your child may get over-excited by the large sum that suddenly lands into their account and decides to use it to buy the latest PlayStation or a weekend in New York!

   The amount of this loan is for the *whole* year but is thankfully delivered to your bank termly.

3. Use a spreadsheet to keep track of your income and outgoings and don't forget to include all the little things as they all add up.

If your child wishes to keep control of their finances and you want to encourage them to budget and take responsibility, UCAS offers some great information and even an online budget calculator.

I have provided you with the necessary link. (guess where!).

CHAPTER 9
THE MOVE

Connecting with Others

Most schools will provide you with a full pack of information about what you need to know before moving. The information given will include accommodation ideas, estate agency numbers, suggestions for doctors' surgeries, dentists and of course, a starter kit list.

Don't worry about having to find a doctor and an a dentist too much, as the school usually recommends where to go and who to see. It's just something to be mindful of, in case your child moves a fair distance from home and won't be able to access their usual doctor or dentist. If your child does find themselves in need of medical help and has not yet registered, tell them not to panic and to speak to their head of year, who will guide them accordingly. This goes for any matter that might be troubling them.

Most schools have their own Facebook page for the new year group. This is a great idea and gives students a chance to get to know each other before starting. The page usually offers lots of information for new starters including clubs, groups and Freshers etc. There is usually access to passes for parties and events which can be paid for online.

It's a good idea for your child to try and meet up with some of the other students beforehand. Pick the pub closest to the drama school and have a bit of lunch.

They may find that they click with someone in particular and hey presto! They've just found their first roommate!

Accommodation

Depending on the school, there may be halls of residence available, which makes life nice and easy for them for the first year. If your talented youngster is under 18, and some schools do take them that young, then you'll find that rooms are available to rent with local host families in the area. If your child isn't going to a university, you'll have to look for some private accommodation. You can find the schools that do and the ones that don't in the beautiful appendix!

Renting accommodation can be the most expensive part, especially if they're studying in London. The best-case scenario is sharing a 3-bed house with a lounge area, but they'll more than likely have to share a 4 bedded house without, as the lounge will most likely have been converted into a bedroom. This is fine, but they won't have a communal space to use. On the positive side, their house is less likely to be the party house! (every cloud!).

Start by contacting local estate agents and remember that at least one of the housemates will have to be available to view the property.

I'm saying this because the chances are that three or four of them will live in different parts of the UK and are not necessarily anywhere near to the drama school.

Another idea is to take turns visiting the areas and liaise between yourselves.

> *Important: Consider the distance from the accommodation to the school.*
>
> *I repeat… Consider the distance from the accommodation to the school.*

Most drama schools or at least the top ones will have a 'no lateness policy'. Late to school? You get sent home for the rest of the day. If your child has to get public transport at six in the morning, it adds huge stress to their already long days.

Drama school (again…the top ones) is like the army. Your child isn't going to have it easy and if they can live a few minutes' walk away from the school instead of a 40-minute bus/train ride, please strongly consider it. As with everything else, the closer the house is, the more expensive it will be. You may find bargain accommodation further afield, but will your child actually make it to lessons?

If you can afford it, it's worth putting more money into closer accommodation and hopefully, you should be able to balance the cost of this, with spending less on transport.

The students will be required to pay the equivalent of a month's rent in advance. This will be on top of the first actual month's rent. They will also have to set up all the household bills. One (reliable) student should be chosen and they will then be named on the bills. A good tip is that if everyone in the house is a full-time student, they won't have to pay council tax. But they do have to remember to apply for it and let the council know as it doesn't happen automatically.

Most students will not yet have a credit score, and this poses a high financial risk to landlords. As a parent, you will probably be required to be a guarantor for the contract period. This is where you'll be glad you went for the 4 bedded room without that lounge and a big party kitchen.

I got away with it lightly. The entire time my son rented, all they needed was a new shower curtain and toilet seat. Along with an iron mark on the carpet and a broken stair rail, that wasn't too bad for what turned out to be four years in the same house with four boys.

Finding a Part-Time Job

This is a difficult one. Should your child get a part-time job whilst studying? I think this depends on their course and timetable.

At universities, the tuition hours are far fewer than at the drama schools, so students will have a fairly clear indication of what free time they have. The chances are that because they've gone to a university, their accommodation will be on campus and they won't have the steep financial cost of renting a private house either.

At the conservatoires, the tuition and contact hours tend to be far greater. Approximately 8 a.m. - 6 p.m. Monday to Friday. The standards are so high that invariably, students choose to stay late to go back over things they have learned and that need perfecting for the next day. They cannot afford to fall behind, or they'll be kicked out. Hard to imagine but this really does happen.

Most students get casual bar work in the local area or shop work if they're lucky, (Some shops don't employ acting students because of their commitment to long hours). If your child drives, working for an Estate Agent is a great option. The hours usually suit and with their acting skills, they make fabulous representatives for the local agencies.

Have a look around, there is usually something that they can make work if they want to.... It's just a matter of fitting it all in!

Let's consider the pros and cons:

PROs

1. Student earns their own money
2. Learns financial independence and responsibility
3. Doesn't drain parents' funds any further
4. Student is contributing

CONs

1. Too tired to work
2. Too busy to work

3. Can't concentrate fully on course and extra-curricular study time to 'keep up'

4. No longer has weekends free to recover for the following week. (honestly, they will need it).

Starter Kit

Before your child starts their course, they should have already purchased the relevant kit. (when I say they, clearly, I mean you) Once they accept the place, they will be sent a starter kit list.

The items on this list can come to around £500, so remember to budget for this. From experience, they don't actually need it all, but I expect you'll get it all just in case… like I did!

I've given you an example kit list in the appendix. At first glance, it might seem straightforward, but unless you live in London, you will probably have to order much of it online.
This is a total pain, as you don't get the luxury of being able to try things on and items like ballet shoes, need quite a specific fit. Let's not even go there, when it comes to sizing dance belts. (basically, a glorified jockstrap… I rest my case!).

If you can visit a shop in person, I would highly recommend you do so. A good time to go is during one of your 'house viewing' weekends in the city of the school.

So that's about it. You've had 6-12 months preparing for the big day and there's not even a wedding to show for it. A jam-packed car (or two) on the journey up and an empty one on the way back. That drive home will be a strange and tearful one (more tissues!).

When you get home, kick your shoes off and pour yourself a glass of bubbly.

Text them fifty times to make sure they are ok and then pat yourself on the back.

You have just done an amazing thing! Your baby has flown the nest and, if you've done your job properly, you can sit back and watch how high they fly. Well done you.

CHAPTER 10
THE BEGINNING

Freshers

Let's be honest, this is basically all about meeting friends and getting drunk. Call me psychic, but I think I know how you're feeling right now…

What if they get so drunk, they choke in the night and you're not there to look after them?

What if, they fall over and break a leg. They won't be able to start the course…and after all this effort!

What if…What if…What if…

They have left the nest remember?
Let go and trust.

Your child is having the time of their lives. They are making new friends and team bonding. They have worked for this place at drama school for years and know full well how much it's cost… not only in money, but in time and commitment. They won't mess up now.

Honestly, please don't worry. The saving grace is that there are timetabled days arranged amongst the alcohol-fuelled havoc of Freshers.

Timetabled days usually include the following:

1. A familiarisation tour of the building(s)

2. An introduction by the Company Principal or Head of Year

3. Distribution of school lanyards/passes, etc.

4. Being partnered up with a 'buddy'

5. Picking a locker, etc.

6. A general jazz/ballet class in order to place the students into the correct set/group for classes. (this is always based on dance rather than acting or singing).

7. Dance discipline

8. Nutrition

9. Allocation of their specific timetable

You see… they'll soon sober up! Of course, all of this is leading to one thing…

DAY 1

This is one occasion, where you can't pre-pack their bag the night before, lay out their clothes on the bed, make a packed lunch, or drop them off. From here on in, they are on their own!

With this in mind, I thought I'd let my son tell you about this bit! (after all, I let him fly, didn't I?)

" So, to be honest, 'day one' started the night before.

After some gentle nudges from mum, telling me to 'pre-pack to save stress in the morning', that's exactly what I did. Bag at the ready, full of everything on the kit list. Clothes laid out, carefully chosen not to look foolish on day one. After all, it's the first day of school all over again.

Other than how to handle my drink and throw together a random fancy dress costume and the drop of a hat, I actually learned a lot through meeting people at Freshers, and some of the older students had recommended that I 'meal prep'. Basically, prepare a meal in a plastic dish and take it in for lunch every day for the next 3 years to save time and money. So, I did just that. Chicken, pasta, and broccoli to be precise!

The morning had arrived, and it was time to get up. Thankfully I'd set about a million alarms to ensure I didn't miss the 8:15 sign in! Imagine getting barred on day one?!

Showered and dressed I was on my way with my 3 housemates (who for the record, 5 years later, are like my brothers), thankful we were only a 12-minute walk away. Obviously we still arrived about half an hour early to be on the safe side.

Much to our disbelief, our head-of-course stood, looming with a stopwatch at the signing-in desk, 'is it really this disciplined?' I thought. We signed in, and went to our first class.

I already had my timetable, so I headed off to lesson one. My timetable was something like this:

1. Acting Class
2. Ballet Class
3. A Break (straight out to suss out where the nearest coffee shop was)
4. Physical Theatre
5. Song Workshop
6. Contextual Studies

It is quite common for students at drama school to run between each lesson. If you're late, you don't

get in, or worse, you go home...end of. So, I ran. Pretty much all the first years did. Luckily the 2nd and 3rd years helped with directions.
I was certainly nervous, but very excited, I loved the atmosphere of the place and even the smell of it.

I was particularly nervous for ballet and jazz as I was absolutely not a dancer, but I couldn't wait for my first singing class, however, that ended in tears (a story for another time) what a loser!
Classes finished at 6 pm (but it would be the first and last time I actually left the building that early.)

My housemates were on different timetables to me, so we left at various times and met back at the house to de-brief. The talent was unreal, and I remember feeling overwhelmed that I was part of this group and had been given such a fantastic chance.

True to my word, I made the obligatory phone call home. I went over everything again and was exhausted by it all. I had an early night in order to cope with day two, but not before, packing my bag, prepping some food, and setting out my clothes, this quickly became my routine! And on the odd occasion, my alarms didn't work at least I was a step ahead to make it in on time.

After looking over my notes from day one, I clambered into bed, set my alarms, and fell straight asleep. Grateful for the amount of support I had from my friends, family, and most of all my mum, to get me there.

Thank God there was no 'Plan B'. "

Conclusion

So, there you have it… from the first conversation to Day One at drama school. I hope this book has provided you with some valuable insights and if it provides even a little clarity for a confused and overwhelmed parent who wants to get it right, then it was worth it.

Just one more thing…

Your child is about to undertake a three-year degree course. It's a tough one. The days are long, and the standards are high. It is physically and emotionally draining, so don't ever let anyone tell you that it's a 'meaningless' degree, a 'namby-pamby' one, or an 'arty-farty' course for non-academic kids! It's more like a cross between the army and an elite sports academy and I dare them to even complete a day of it.

As a parent, it was quite an eye-opener at how hard

the students worked and how dedicated they were. There were tearful phone calls home and many days of self-doubt, but there were also days of pure excitement, achievement, and pride.

There were also phone calls home to tell me he was going to be singing at the Albert Hall with John Barrowman and at the 'Oliviers' with Audra McDonald and he had just met Andrew Lloyd Webber in the corridor! As a parent, these were the calls I loved the most and which made the process so worthwhile.

I have absolutely no regrets about selling my soul to send him to drama school. It wasn't really that bad, with careful planning, saving and cutting out holidays for a few years (6 actually!) we managed to come up with the money.

I have to say at this stage, a large amount of the money came from my Son's own savings. Eighteen years of his birthday and Christmas money from relatives was used to help achieve his dream, so I can't fault him for that, and I expect that may have made him even more determined to succeed.

Remember the interview part of this book?

When my son had his interview on his audition day, he was asked what he was hoping to get from attending the drama school. His reply was "Get me into 'The Book of Mormon". (May as well aim high, he thought!)

My son survived the full three-year course and graduated with a BA(Hons) in Musical Theatre. The very next day after leaving school, he was signed to a musical called 'Heathers' that within months, transferred to London's West End. (I do believe this was the first popping of a champagne bottle since his offer letter!)

After completing a panto season at the amazing Liverpool Empire as 'Jack' in Jack in the Beanstalk, he was offered another job.

He is currently on tour with 'The Book of Mormon".

I have goose bumps even writing this.

So, with this book in hand, go ahead and secure that dream. It can be done, even the funding.

Good luck or should I say, 'break a leg'. I hope this book serves you well.

THE APPENDIX

25 Drama Schools

Schools Currently Offering Dance & Drama Awards

Helpful Funding Websites

Links to Non-School Associated Bursaries

Sample of Personal Statement

Example Starter Kit Requirements

Sample Funding Application Letter

Performing Arts CV

Links to Other Useful Websites

25 DRAMA SCHOOLS

The following 25 schools have been listed in alphabetical order and in no way represent any order of personal or industry opinion.

For ease of use, I have used details that represent a 3-year course in Musical Theatre or Acting. There may be slight differences if you chose a different type of course.

There are three blank tables for you to fill in yourself if you are considering a school that is not included here.

At the time of publishing, most schools were being affected by the COVID-19 outbreak and were holding their open days/auditions and classes online. This is made clear on their websites. The information used reflects their usual manner of operation.

Here we go...

INCLUDED IN THIS SECTION
(In alphabetical order)

Academy of Live & Recorded Arts (ALRA)
Arts Educational Schools London, The (ArtsEd)
Bird College
Bristol Old Vic Theatre School
E15 Acting School (E15)
Emil Dale Academy (EDA)
Guildford School of Acting (GSA)
Guildhall School of Music & Drama
Italia Conti Academy of Theatre Arts
Laine Theatre Arts (Laines)
Liverpool Institute for Performing Arts (LIPA)
London Academy of Music & Dramatic Art (LAMDA)
Manchester School of Theatre (MMU)
Mountview Acedemy of Theatre Arts
Oxford School of Drama
Performers College
Rose Bruford College of Theatre & Performance
Royal Academy of Dramatic Art (RADA)
Royal Birmingham Conservatoire
Royal Central School of Speech & Drama, The (Central)
Royal Conservatoire of Scotland, The (RCS)
Royal Welsh College of Music & Drama, The (RWCMD)
Stella Mann College of Performing Arts
University of Chichester
Urdang Academy, The

Academy of Live and Recorded Arts (ALRA)
Two Sites in Greater Manchester and London
Tel: 01942 821021 (Manchester) Tel: 020 8870 6475 (London)

Website Address	www.alra.co.uk
Nearest Train/Tube Station	Wigan North or Tooting Bec
Courses Available	Acting
Open Days	Autumn (on days of productions)
How to Apply	Directly to the school
Application Deadline	May
Admission Requirements	Audition
Audition Fee	£35 Manchester £45 London
Audition Procedure	All in one day - No recalls
Course Fees (per year)	£10,500 (Man) £13,900 (Lon)
Student Loan Available	Partial
BA (Hons) Available	Yes
Bursaries/Scholarships Available	Yes
School Offers Accommodation	No

Notable Alumni

Sarah Parish, Tanya Franks, Miranda Hart, Jimmy Akingbola

NOTES

The Arts Educational Schools, London (ArtsEd)

Bath Road, Chiswick, W4
Tel: 020 8987 6666

Website Address	www.artsed.co.uk
Nearest Train/Tube Station	Turnham Green
Courses Available	Acting, Musical Theatre
Open Days	No - Audition Day Only
How to Apply	Directly to the school
Application Deadline	March
Admission Requirements	Audition (2 A Levels & 5 GCSEs desirable)
Audition Fee	£45
Audition Procedure	Audition, Recall & Interview on the same day. Approx. 1 week wait for results.
Course Fees (per year)	£15,360
Student Loan Available	Partial
BA (Hons) Available	Yes - £548
Bursaries/Scholarships Available	Yes
School Offers Accommodation	No

Notable Alumni

Dame Julie Andrews, Samantha Barks, Darcey Bussell, Adam Cooper, Martin Clunes, Nigel Havers, Bonnie Langford, Will Young

NOTES

Bird College
Alma Road, Sidcup, Kent, DA14 4ED
Tel: 020 8300 6004

Website Address	www.bird-college.com
Nearest Train/Tube Station	Sidcup
Courses Available	Professional Dance & Musical Theatre
Open Days	September, October & January
How to Apply	Via UCAS & directly to school within 10 days of each other
Application Deadline	End January
Admission Requirements	64 UCAS Points at A-Level, 2 x AS Levels & Audition
Audition Fee	£45
Audition Procedure	Act, sing, dance, physio & interview on the same day. Approx. 3-4 week wait for results
Course Fees (per year)	£9,500
Student Loan Available	Full
BA (Hons) Available	Yes
Bursaries/Scholarships Available	Yes
School Offers Accommodation	Host Families for those under 18 Onsite Campus for Year 1 (18+)

Notable Alumni

Lara Pulver, John Partridge, Melanie Chisholm

NOTES

Bristol Old Vic Theatre School
1-3 Downside Road, Clifton, Bristol, BS8 2XF
Tel: 0117 973 3535

Website Address	www.bristololdvic.org.uk
Nearest Train/Tube Station	Bristol Temple Meads
Courses Available	Professional Acting, Production, Film & TV
Open Days	October
How to Apply	Via UCAS
Application Deadline	Mid-January
Admission Requirements	2 A-Levels or equivalent
Audition Fee	£25
Audition Procedure	Audition & Recall Workshop
Course Fees (per year)	£9,250
Student Loan Available	Full
BA (Hons) Available	Yes
Bursaries/Scholarships Available	Yes
School Offers Accommodation	No

Notable Alumni

Helen Baxendale, Olivia Colman, Sir Daniel Day-Lewis, Jeremy Irons, Amanda Redman, Miranda Richardson

NOTES

East 15 Acting School (E15)

Hatfields, Rectory Lane, Loughton, IG10 3RY
Tel: 020 8508 5983

Website Address	www.east15.ac.uk
Nearest Train/Tube Station	Debden
Courses Available	Acting, Acting & Contemporary Theatre, Acting & Community Theatre, Acting & Stage Combat, Physical Theatre
Open Days	Yes
How to Apply	Via UCAS & directly to the school
Application Deadline	Mid Jan/ (UCAS)/End of June
Admission Requirements	Audition
Audition Fee	£55
Audition Procedure	Same day
Course Fees (per year)	£9,250
Student Loan Available	Full
BA (Hons) Available	Yes
Bursaries/Scholarships Available	Yes
School Offers Accomodation	No

Notable Alumni

Alison Steadman, Damon Albarn, David Yip, Marc Warren

NOTES

Emil Dale Academy (EDA)

60 Wilbury Way, Hitchin, Hertfordshire, SG4 0TP
Tel: 01462 677 808

Website Address	www.emildale.co.uk
Nearest Train/Tube Station	Hitchin
Courses Available	Professional Musical Theatre
Open Days	September
How to Apply	Directly to the School
Application Deadline	None - Applications close when audition spaces are full
Admission Requirements	Audition/80 UCAS points desirable
Audition Fee	£35
Audition Procedure	Audition, Jazz Class & Interview
Course Fees (per year)	£12,250
Student Loan Available	Full
BA (Hons) Available	Yes
Bursaries/Scholarships Available	Yes
School Offers Accommodation	Student housing and host families available

Notable Alumni

Aaron Thomas Ward, Jack Churms, Joseph Peacock

NOTES

Guildford School of Acting (GSA)

Stag Hill, University Campus, Guildford GU2 7XH
Tel: 01483 682222

Website Address	www.gsauk.org
Nearest Train/Tube Station	Guildford
Courses Available	Acting, Acting Musicianship, Dance, Musical Theatre
Open Days	September - October
How to Apply	Via UCAS
Application Deadline	Mid-January
Admission Requirements	Audition (However, 2A-Levels & 5 GCSEs desirable)
Audition Fee	£55
Audition Procedure	Recall same day + additional
Course Fees (per year)	£9,250
Student Loan Available	Full
BA (Hons) Available	Yes
Bursaries/Scholarships Available	Yes
School Offers Accommodation	On-campus accommodation for 1st year

Notable Alumni

Bill Deamer, Tom Chambers, Blenda Blethyn, Emma Barton, Michael Ball, Caroline Sheen, Jodie Steele

NOTES

Guildhall School of Music and Drama
Silk Street, Barbican, EC2Y 8DT
Tel: 020 7628 2571

Website Address	www.gsmd.ac.uk
Nearest Train/Tube Station	Moorgate
Courses Available	Technical Arts, Production Arts, Video Design for Live Performance, Performance & Creative Enterprise, Acting
Open Days	September & December
How to Apply	Directly to the school
Application Deadline	January
Admission Requirements	Application & Audition
Audition Fee	Currently £35 - Auditions held in major cities nationwide (Usually £66)
Audition Procedure	1st Audition regionally, 2nd audition in London, Recalls usually in May
Course Fees (per year)	£9,250
Student Loan Available	Full
BA (Hons) Available	Yes
Bursaries/Scholarships Available	Yes
School Offers Accommodation	No

Notable Alumni

Daniel Craig, Lily James, Ewan McGregor, Sarah Lancashire, Lesley Sharp, Jodie Whittaker

NOTES

Italia Conti Academy of Theatre Arts

Italia Conti House, 23 Goswell Road, Barbican, London, EC1M 7AJ
Tel: 0207 608 0044

Website Address	www.italiaconti.com
Nearest Train/Tube Station	Barbican
Courses Available	Acting, Musical Theatre October, November & January
Open Days	October, November & January
How to Apply	Via UCAS
Application Deadline	Mid-January
Admission Requirements	Application & Audition
Audition Fee	£45
Audition Procedure	Act, Sing, Dance, Interview on same day
Course Fees (per year)	£9,250
Student Loan Available	Full
BA (Hons) Available	Yes
Bursaries/Scholarships Available	Yes
School Offers Accommodation	No

Notable Alumni

Sam Tutty, Layton Williams, Tracie Bennett, Pixie Lott

NOTES

Laine Theatre Arts (Laines)
The Studios, East Street, Epsom, Surrey KT17 1HH
Tel: 01372 724648

Website Address	www.laine-theatre-arts.co.uk
Nearest Train/Tube Station	Epsom
Courses Available	Musical Theatre
Open Days	October
How to Apply	Directly to the school
Application Deadline	31st January
Admission Requirements	Audition
Audition Fee	£45
Audition Procedure	Dance & Acting Workshops + solos
Course Fees (per year)	£9,000
Student Loan Available	No
BA (Hons) Available	Yes
Bursaries/Scholarships Available	Yes
School Offers Accommodation	No

Notable Alumni

Charlie Stemp, Gary Lloyd

NOTES

Liverpool Institute for Performing Arts (LIPA)
Mount Street, Liverpool, L1 9HF
Tel: 0151 3303000

Website Address	www.lipa.ac.uk
Nearest Train/Tube Station	Liverpool Lime Street
Courses Available	Acting, Acting & Screen, Dance, Music, Theatre Design
Open Days	June
How to Apply	Via UCAS *and* directly to the school
Application Deadline	Mid-January
Admission Requirements	5 x C Grade GCSEs, 64 UCAS points & Audition
Audition Fee	£40
Audition Procedure	Audition. Result via UCAS
Course Fees (per year)	£9,250
Student Loan Available	Full
BA (Hons) Available	Yes
Bursaries/Scholarships Available	Yes
School Offers Accommodation	No

Notable Alumni

Evie Pickerill, Leanne Best, Lisa Stokke, Madeline Appiah

NOTES

London Academy of Music and Dramatic Art (LAMDA)

155 Talgarth Road, London, W14 9DA
Tel: 020 8834 0500

Website Address	www.lamda.ac.uk
Nearest Train/Tube Station	Barons Court
Courses Available	Acting, Production & Technical Arts
Open Days	No
How to Apply	Directly to school
Application Deadline	March
Admission Requirements	Audition
Audition Fee	Initial Audition, Recall £48
Audition Procedure	Group workshop & Interview - Results in 2 weeks. Recall at a later date with results in 2-3 weeks.
Course Fees (per year)	£9,250
Student Loan Available	Full
BA (Hons) Available	Yes
Bursaries/Scholarships Available	Yes
School Offers Accommodation	Yes

Notable Alumni

Jim Broadbent, Julie Hesmondhalgh, Benedict Cumberbatch

NOTES

Manchester School of Theatre (MMU)
70 Oxford Street, Manchester M1 5NH
Tel: 0161 247 1306

Website Address	www.theatre.mmu.ac.uk
Nearest Train/Tube Station	Manchester Oxford Road
Courses Available	Acting, Drama & Contemporary Performance
Open Days	Yes, October & November
How to Apply	Via UCAS
Application Deadline	Mid-January
Admission Requirements	Audition
Audition Fee	£45
Audition Procedure	Recalls on a separate day
Course Fees (per year)	£9,250
Student Loan Available	Full
BA (Hons) Available	Yes
Bursaries/Scholarships Available	No
School Offers Accommodation	Yes

Notable Alumni

Dame Julie Walters, Victoria Wood, Steve Coogan, Amanda Burton, John Thomson

NOTES

Mountview Academy of Theatre Arts
120 Peckham Hill Street, London, SE15 5JT
Tel: 020 8881 2201

Website Address	www.mountview.org.uk
Nearest Train/Tube Station	Wood Green
Courses Available	Acting, Actor Musicianship, Musical Theatre
Open Days	No - Only for Theatre Production
How to Apply	Directly to the school
Application Deadline	December
Admission Requirements	Audition (2 A Levels & 5 GCSEs desirable)
Audition Fee	£35-45
Audition Procedure	Regional auditions are available. Recall & Interview on a separate day, with approx. 1 week wait for results
Course Fees (per year)	£14,700
Student Loan Available	Partial
BA (Hons) Available	Yes - £505
Bursaries/Scholarships Available	Yes
School Offers Accommodation	Yes

Notable Alumni

Connie Fisher, Amanda Holden, Glynis Barber, Cleve September

NOTES

Oxford School of Drama
Sansomes Farm Studios, Woodstock, Oxfordshire, OX20 1ER
Tel: 01993 812883

Website Address	www.oxforddrama.ac.uk
Nearest Train/Tube Station	Tackley
Courses Available	Acting
Open Days	Yes
How to Apply	Directly to school
Application Deadline	End of May
Admission Requirements	Audition
Audition Fee	£45
Audition Procedure	Recalls on a separate day
Course Fees (per year)	£17,200
Student Loan Available	Partial
BA (Hons) Available	No, but is equivalent to a degree
Bursaries/Scholarships Available	Yes
School Offers Accommodation	No

Notable Alumni

Christina Cole, Claire Foy, Lee Boardman

NOTES

Performers College

Southend Road, Corringham, Essex SS17 8JS
Tel: 01375 672053

Website Address	www.perfromerscollege.co.uk
Nearest Train/Tube Station	Basildon
Courses Available	Musical Theatre & Dance
Open Days	November
How to Apply	Directly to the school
Application Deadline	End of January
Admission Requirements	Audition/3 x A Levels
Audition Fee	No
Audition Procedure	Audition
Course Fees (per year)	£9,250
Student Loan Available	Full
BA (Hons) Available	Yes
Bursaries/Scholarships Available	Yes
School Offers Accommodation	No

Notable Alumni

Dougie Mills, Gary Wood, Joe Pegram

NOTES

Rose Bruford College of Theatre & Performance
Lamorbey Park, Burnt Oak Lane, Sidcup, Kent, DA15 9DF
Tel: 020 8308 2600

Website Address	www.bruford.ac.uk
Nearest Train/Tube Station	Sidcup
Courses Available	Acting, Acting Musicianship
Open Days	October
How to Apply	Via UCAS
Application Deadline	Mid-January
Admission Requirements	Audition/64 UCAS points
Audition Fee	£55 Although there are many exemptions
Audition Procedure	Recalls on a separate day
Course Fees (per year)	£9,250
Student Loan Available	Full
BA (Hons) Available	Yes
Bursaries/Scholarships Available	Yes
School Offers Accommodation	No

Notable Alumni

Anthony Daniels, Gary Oldman, Maddy Hill

NOTES

Royal Academy of Dramatic Arts (RADA)
62-64 Gower Street, London, WC1E 6ED
Tel: 020 7636 7076

Website Address	www.rada.ac.uk
Nearest Train/Tube Station	Goodge street
Courses Available	Acting, Technical Theatre & Stage Management
Open Days	No
How to Apply	Directly to the school
Application Deadline	November - February
Admission Requirements	N/A
Audition Fee	Initial Audition £12, Recall £48
Audition Procedure	Recalls on a separate day
Course Fees (per year)	£9,000
Student Loan Available	Full
BA (Hons) Available	Yes
Bursaries/Scholarships Available	Yes
School Offers Accommodation	No

Notable Alumni

Dame Joan Collins, Peter O'Toole, Kenneth Branagh, Alan Rickman, Sir John Gielgud, Ben Whishaw, Michael Sheen

NOTES

Royal Birmingham Conservatoire

200 Jennens Road, Birmingham, B4 7XR
Tel: 0121 3315000

Website Address	www.bru.ac.uk
Nearest Train/Tube Station	Bull Street
Courses Available	Acting, Applied Theatre
Open Days	Yes
How to Apply	Via UCAS
Application Deadline	Mid-January
Admission Requirements	Audition
Audition Fee	£46
Audition Procedure	Audition & interview. Recalls on a separate day
Course Fees (per year)	£9,250
Student Loan Available	Full
BA (Hons) Available	Yes
Bursaries/Scholarships Available	Yes
School Offers Accommodation	Yes

Notable Alumni

Helen George, Jimi Mistry, Tom Lister

NOTES

The Royal Central School of Speech and Drama (Central)

Eton Avenue, London, NW3 3HY, UK
Tel: 020 7722 8183

Website Address	www.cssd.ac.uk
Nearest Train/Tube Station	Swiss Cottage
Courses Available	Acting, Musical Theatre
Open Days	Only for technical courses
How to Apply	Directly to school
Application Deadline	End of February (£46 -76 Application Fee)
Admission Requirements	Audition
Audition Fee	£46-76 depending on the date
Audition Procedure	Four stage process of Workshops & Solos & Recalls
Course Fees (per year)	£9,000
Student Loan Available	Full
BA (Hons) Available	Yes £1000
Bursaries/Scholarships Available	Yes
School Offers Accommodation	No

Notable Alumni

Dame Judy Dench, Christopher Eccleston, Martin Freeman, Dawn French, Sir Cameron Mackintosh, James Nesbitt, Zoe Wannamaker

NOTES

Royal Conservatoire of Scotland, The (RCS)
100 Renfrew Street, Glasgow, G2 3DB
Tel: 0141 3324101

Website Address	www.rcs.ac.uk
Nearest Train/Tube Station	Glasgow Queen Street or Glasgow Central
Courses Available	Modern Ballet, Acting, Contemporary Performance, Music, Musical Theatre
Open Days	October
How to Apply	Via UCAS
Application Deadline	Mid-January
Admission Requirements	£26 Application Fee
Audition Fee	£55
Audition Procedure	Same Day
Course Fees (per year)	£9,250 (£1820 Scottish Students)
Student Loan Available	Full
BA (Hons) Available	Yes
Bursaries/Scholarships Available	Yes
School Offers Accommodation	No

Notable Alumni

Alan Cumming, Richard Madden, David Tennant, Ruby Wax, James McAvoy, Laura Donnelly, Robert Carlyle

NOTES

Royal Welsh College of Music & Drama (RWCMD)

Castle Grounds, Cathays Park, Cardiff, CF10 3ER
Tel: 029 2034 2854

Website Address	www.rwcmd.ac.uk
Nearest Train/Tube Station	Cardiff
Courses Available	Acting, Musical Theatre, Stage Management & Technical Theatre
Open Days	June
How to Apply	Via UCAS
Application Deadline	Mid-January
Admission Requirements	Application & Audition
Audition Fee	£35
Audition Procedure	At the college in March & April. Recalls on a separate day
Course Fees (per year)	£9,000
Student Loan Available	Full
BA (Hons) Available	Yes
Bursaries/Scholarships Available	Yes
School Offers Accommodation	Yes, for Year one - Must meet the application deadline

Notable Alumni

Sir Anthony Hopkins, Eve Myles, Rob Brydon, Jo Joyner, Dougray Scott

NOTES

Stella Mann College of Performing Arts

10 Linden Rd, Bedford, MK40 2DA
Tel: 01234 213331

Website Address	www.stellamanncollege.co.uk
Nearest Train/Tube Station	Bedford
Courses Available	Musical Theatre, Dance
Open Days	Yes
How to Apply	Directly to the school
Application Deadline	August
Admission Requirements	Audition & Interview
Audition Fee	£35
Audition Procedure	Ballet & Jazz classes, Physio, solos & Interview
Course Fees (per year)	£10,275
Student Loan Available	Partial - Up to £9,250 No maintenance loans available
BA (Hons) Available	Yes
Bursaries/Scholarships Available	Yes
School Offers Accommodation	No

Notable Alumni

Janet Montgomery

NOTES

The University of Chichester
College Lane, Chichester, West Sussex, PO19 6PE
Tel: 01243 816000

Website Address	www.chi.ac.uk
Nearest Train/Tube Station	Chichester
Courses Available	Acting, Acting for Film, Drama, Theatre & Directing, Music & Musical Theatre, Musical Theatre (Triple Threat) & More
Open Days	June, October & November
How to Apply	Via UCAS
Application Deadline	Mid-January
Admission Requirements	Audition & 3 A Levels
Audition Fee	No
Audition Procedure	Act, Sing, Dance & Q&A in one day
Course Fees (per year)	£9,250
Student Loan Available	Full
BA (Hons) Available	Yes
Bursaries/Scholarships Available	Yes
School Offers Accommodation	Yes - Apply before June to guarantee a place

Notable Alumni

Alun Davies, Jason Merrells

NOTES

The Urdang Academy

The Old Finsbury Town Hall, Rosebery Avenue, London, EC1R 4RP
Tel: 020 7713 7710

Website Address	www.theurdang.london
Nearest Train/Tube Station	Covent Garden
Courses Available	Professional Dance & Musical Theatre,
Open Days	Yes
How to Apply	Via UCAS
Application Deadline	Mid-January
Admission Requirements	Audition/4 x GCSEs 80 UCAS points
Audition Fee	£45
Audition Procedure	An emailed response. Recall at a later date
Course Fees (per year)	£9,250
Student Loan Available	Full
BA (Hons) Available	Yes
Bursaries/Scholarships Available	Yes
School Offers Accommodation	No

Notable Alumni

Allison Carroll, Amber Davies, Victoria Hamilton-Barritt

NOTES

Website Address	
Nearest Train/Tube Station	
Courses Available	
Open Days	
How to Apply	
Application Deadline	
Admission Requirements	
Audition Fee	
Audition Procedure	
Course Fees (per year)	
Student Loan Available	
BA (Hons) Available	
Bursaries/Scholarships Available	
School Offers Accommodation	

Notable Alumni

NOTES

Website Address	
Nearest Train/Tube Station	
Courses Available	
Open Days	
How to Apply	
Application Deadline	
Admission Requirements	
Audition Fee	
Audition Procedure	
Course Fees (per year)	
Student Loan Available	
BA (Hons) Available	
Bursaries/Scholarships Available	
School Offers Accommodation	

Notable Alumni

NOTES

SCHOOLS CURRENTLY OFFERING DANCE AND DRAMA AWARDS

Arts.Ed, London
Bird College
Elmhurst Ballet School
English National Ballet School
The Hammond School
Italia Conti Arts Centre
KS Dance
Laine Theatre Arts
Liverpool Theatre School
Mountview Academy of Theatre Arts
Northern Ballet School
The Oxford School of Drama
Performers College
SLP College Leeds
Stella Mann College

Schools in **bold** are included in this book.

HELPFUL FUNDING WEBSITES

Check out the Student loan site for your country for full and up to date details:

ENGLAND
www.gov.uk/apply-online-for-student-finance

WALES
www.studentfinancewales.co.uk

SCOTLAND
www.mygov.scot/apply-student-loan/

NORTHERN IRELAND
www.studentfinanceni.co.uk

UCAS Online Budget Calculator
www.ucas.com/budget-calculator

Money Advice Services - Savings Calculator
www.moneyadviceservices.org.uk

LINKS TO NON-SCHOOL RELATED BURSARIES

www.gov.uk/1619-bursary-fund
Bursaries to help with education-related costs if you're aged 16 to 19 and studying at a publicly funded school or college in England - not a university.

www.thescholarshiphub.org.uk
The Scholarship Hub includes funds offered by universities themselves, companies, charities, trusts, and other organisations, as well as information on sponsored degrees and degree apprenticeships.

www.nationalyouthartstrust.org.uk/what-we-do/bursaries/
Bursaries are available for music, dance, and drama of up to £1000 for students up to 25 years of age.

www.crowdscholar.co.uk
University scholarships for the UK's most promising students from disadvantaged backgrounds.

www.leverhulme.ac.uk/arts-scholarships
For specialist arts institutions or registered charities to provide training opportunities across the fine and performing arts.

www.leathersellers.co.uk/charitablefund/
Provides a wide range of funding to UK registered Charities, Educational Institutions, and University Students.

www.fundingforall.org.uk/funds/the-mackintosh-foundation/
Promoting and developing theatrical, musical, and dramatic arts by a variety of means including education.

www.williambarrytrust.org.uk/home.html

To advance the education and vocational training of persons engaged or about to engage in technical craft and artistic occupations in particular.

www.thesidney-perry-foundation.co.uk
You are advised not to apply until you have a confirmed college placement and a full understanding of the costs involved. Enclose proof of your offer.

SAMPLE PERSONAL STATEMENT

Start with a strong and straight-to-the-point opener:

I understand fully, that the career I have chosen is one of the hardest, but I remain eager to succeed and am excited at the prospect of soaking up the specialist training being offered by **NAME OF SCHOOL** and using this training as a springboard for my success in the industry. I am ready to apply myself fully to this course, both physically and emotionally, and am anticipating a disciplined and hard-working environment, which in turn will help me to progress further and help me reach my full potential.

Now include a little about your experience:

Extensive experience in performing arts has enabled me to enjoy playing a variety of roles, including **NAME OF BEST ROLES**. The part of **NAME OF PART HERE** has been my greatest learning curve regards acting because **STATE REASON HERE**.

Show them that you are actively researching and immersing yourself in the arts:

I try to experience a diverse range of plays and musical theatre, either live, recorded, or online, the latest of which, was **NAME OF PRODUCTION** at **NAME OF THEATRE**, starring **NAME OF ACTOR**. I especially enjoy the work of **FAVOURITE PERFORMER (STATE WHAT THEY HAVE BEEN IN)**. Their work has not only influenced me as a performer but has also **EXPLAIN HERE**

Currently, the music I listen to most includes the work of **NAME OF COMPOSER**, whose music I have admired for some time now, especially **NAME A MUSICAL NUMBER**. I would like to think that as part of the 3-year training course, my knowledge of composers, lyricists, and new musicals will increase even more.

Time to brag about any special awards or achievements:

My commitment to Performing Arts was rewarded in **YEAR** when I received **NAME OF AWARD/ACHIEVEMENT** and I was thrilled to receive 'A' grades in my recent Music and Drama exams, including full marks for my Shakespearian monologue and maximum marks in my practical music exam where my chosen instrument was my voice. (**CHANGE AS NECESSARY**)

Now for a positive and committed finisher:

Being fully aware of the pitfalls of the industry, I know full well the amount of hard work and dedication that will be expected of me. I want you to know that I have the energy and commitment required to undertake your training and ultimately, a career in the musical theatre industry. I believe that the course being offered by **NAME OF SCHOOL** would provide me with the best possible tuition, which in turn, will help me reach my long-term ambition of performing professionally.

You should now be at approx. 500 words, so edit and proofread before submitting and don't forget to change the name of the school throughout the statement each time you send it to a new school - It's easily done and will undermine all your clever words.

* Careful not to copy this verbatim, you're not the only one to be reading this book (Well at least I hope you're not!) and the schools don't want thousands of the same statement!

EXAMPLE STARTER KIT REQUIREMENTS

Women
2 x Leotards
2 X Black Tights
2 X Pairs of ballet flats
1 x Pair of soft Ballet blocks
1 x Pair of tap shoes
1 x Pair of split sole shoes with heels
1 x Pair of split sole jazz trainer
1 x Pair of split sole jazz shoes
1 x Crop top
3 X Pairs of black hot pants
1 full, calf-length practice skirt
1 x White shirt
1 x Pair knee pads
2 Pairs of food thongs
1 x Sweat towel

Men
2 x Leotards or tight-fitting vests
2 x Pairs of footless tights
2 x Pairs of black dance shorts
1 x Pair of tap shoes
2 x Pairs of black canvas ballet flats
2 Dance supports
1 x Pair of split sole jazz trainer

1 x Pair of split sole jazz shoes
1 x Pair of black formal shoes
1 x Pair of black formal trousers
1 White shirt
1 x Pair of knee pads
2 x Pairs of foot thongs
1 x Sweat towel

All Students
Jogging bottoms & Loose warm sweaters (for voice classes)
Books as specified
A recording device (Most students use their phones)
Ice packs
A TheraBand
A Padlock & Key
Stationery - Pencils, highlighters, erasers, Sellotape, poly pockets, ring binders, etc.

Not forgetting a sturdy holdall, sportsbag or backpack to house it all in.

FUNDING APPLICATION LETTER

Dear Sirs (unless you have an actual name),

Let's start with a brief overview of who you are and why you are writing:

My name is **NAME,** I am **AGE** years old and have been extremely fortunate at successfully auditioning for, and subsequently being offered, an unconditional place at the prestigious **NAME OF DRAMA SCHOOL.** I am due to start the 3-year (BA Hons) **NAME OF COURSE** in September this year and it is with this in mind, that I am applying to the trust for potential funding

Tell the Trust how excellent your chosen school is:

NAME OF SCHOOL is one of the top conservatoires in the country for Musical Theatre training and offers approximately 30-40 places each year after auditioning thousands. After the vigorous but rewarding training, the conservatoire proudly reports that 100% of their graduates leave with agent representation and an astounding 95% of graduates are offered professional work within six months of leaving. In the performing arts profession, this is almost unheard of, and I am therefore under no illusion as to how fortunate I am to have been offered a place, and am determined to find the funds to enable me to accept this fantastic opportunity and to attend this prestigious school.

Tell them how much it's going to cost:

The annual tuition fee for the course is **COST OF COURSE PER YEAR** and as it is a privately-run school, I am not able to secure a full student loan. In addition to this, I need to budget for rent and living expenses whilst living in **CITY OF SCHOOL** for the duration of the course.

What have you done to raise funds already?

To date, I have managed to save **AMOUNT** by various means, including taking a part-time job, selling my car, and singing for high profile events in the local area. I am in the process of organising a musical theatre evening and recording a CD which I hope will raise further funds! Despite my efforts, I am mindful I will still have a considerable shortfall. **(ADAPT AS NECESSARY)**

Time to brag about your achievements to date - Why do you deserve to receive funding from the trust?

Before the trust is to even consider my application, I should perhaps, tell you a little about myself:

I have been performing in Musical Theatre from the age of **AGE (THIS IS OK HERE BUT NOT FOR YOUR PERSONAL STATEMENT)** and whilst at senior school was heavily involved with both the music and drama departments. I played many principal roles in the school productions and my commitment was rewarded in **YEAR** when I received the 'Performing Arts award for outstanding contribution to music and drama'. **(OR WHATEVER)**

In **YEAR**, I was chosen to/chosen for/Had the opportunity to/Had the experience of **SPECIFY**. I feel this experience went some way in contributing towards my subsequent audition success at **NAME OF SCHOOL**.

TALK ABOUT YOUR LOCAL THEATRE SCHOOL/DRAMA CLASSES/BEST ROLES HERE

ANY MUSIC LESSONS/VOCAL COACHING/CHOIR EXPERIENCE HERE

TALK ABOUT ANY VOLUNTARY WORK HERE

Time to be passionate and let the trust know how committed you are to make this happen:

I understand fully, that the career I have chosen is one of the hardest, but I remain eager to succeed and am excited at the prospect of soaking up the specialist training being offered by **NAME OF DRAMA SCHOOL** and using this training as a springboard for my success in the industry.

I am ready to apply myself fully to this course, both physically and emotionally, and am anticipating a disciplined and hard-working environment, which in turn will help me reach my full potential.

And finally…

If the trust should see fit to offer me any amount of financial assistance, I want you to know that I will work hard and fully commit to the course. This wonderful opportunity will provide me with the best possible tuition, which in turn, will help me reach my long-term ambition of performing professionally. If this could be aided in any way by **NAME OF TRUST**, then you need to know that I would be forever appreciative.

Oops! Don't forget this little finisher:

Please find enclosed my Performing Arts CV, my headshot, and a stamped address envelope for your reply, which will be most appreciated.

Yours faithfully,
NAME

PERFORMING ARTS CV

YEAR	Name of Production	Part Played	Theatre Company
YEAR	Name of Production	Part Played	Theatre Company
YEAR	Name of Production	Part Played	Theatre Company
YEAR	Name of Production	Part Played	Theatre Company
YEAR	Name of Production	Part Played	Theatre Company
YEAR	Name of Production	Part Played	Theatre Company
YEAR	Name of Production	Part Played	Theatre Company
YEAR	Name of Production	Part Played	Theatre Company
YEAR	Name of Production	Part Played	Theatre Company

Names and addresses of suggested references should you need them:

1. NAME
ADDRESS
ADDRESS

2. NAME
ADDRESS
ADDRESS

LINKS TO OTHER USEFUL WEBSITES

The National Youth Theatre (NYT)
For young people aged 14-25
www.nyt.org.uk

The National Youth Music Theatre (NYMT)
For young people aged 16-23
www.nymt.org.uk

Actors & Performers Yearbook
Revised and updated each year, this book includes approximately 60 pages of information on training and drama schools.
www.actorsandperformers.com

National Union of Students
This is a great site for your child to peruse and offers loads of advice and discounts.
www.nus.org.uk

Switch Words by Liz Dean
Might these words help you beat your audition nerves? Give it a go!
http://lizdean.info/switchwords-2/

Preparing Your Audition Piano Music
https://www.youtube.com/watch?v=3uHj9bskzYo

Acknowledgements

Thanks to the parents of my own pupils past and present whose experiences and feedback helped shape this book, to Andrea Daly-Dickson for her help in preparing the book prior to publishing, to everyone that contributed and enabled my own son to get to drama school and most of all, to Alex James-Hatton for sharing his dream with me!

*****

Please Leave a Review

As an independent author, I am indebted to loyal readers (like you) for spreading the word about my book and helping to get it into the hands of those who would really benefit from it. I would therefore be grateful if you could spend just a couple of minutes leaving a review (it can be as short as you like!) on the Amazon website, my Google Page or my Facebook page.

Thank you so much!

Amanda

Coming Soon...

For a valuable insight into what a 3-year course is like and what to expect, you'll want to read the next book in this series:

So, Your Child is at DRAMA SCHOOL?

The book is an insightful look at the whole three years at drama school, from the first lessons, allocation of sets and stressful phone calls home, to headshots, end of year shows and getting an agent. In fact, this book takes you all the way through to graduation day and to your child signing their first contract.

A must-read for any parent. (or student for that matter!)

*****

ABOUT THE AUTHOR

Originally from Hertfordshire, Amanda relocated to Wales when her son was five. She is a trained dance teacher & choreographer, runs an award-winning musical theatre academy, a talent management agency, and can even be found on screen in a couple of films. (careful not to blink or you'll miss her!)

Apart from her theatrical endeavours, you can usually find Amanda painting or playing Scrabble!

www.amandabcosgrove.co.uk

  amandabcosgrove

  amandabcosgrove

  amandabcosgrove

Printed in Poland
by Amazon Fulfillment
Poland Sp. z o.o., Wrocław